[NATIVE AMERICAN NATIONS]

Wampanoag

F.A. BIRD

Checkerboard
Library

An Imprint of Abdo Publishing
abdobooks.com

ABDOBOOKS.COM

Published by Abdo Publishing, a division of ABDO, PO Box 398166, Minneapolis, Minnesota 55439. Copyright © 2025 by Abdo Consulting Group, Inc. International copyrights reserved in all countries. No part of this book may be reproduced in any form without written permission from the publisher. Checkerboard Library™ is a trademark and logo of Abdo Publishing.

Printed in the United States of America, North Mankato, Minnesota
102024
012025

Editor: Lauri Nelson
Design: Mighty Media, Inc.

Cover Photograph: Essdras M Suarez/The Boston Globe/Getty Images
Interior Photographs: Ad_hominem/Shutterstock Images, p. 7; Angel Wynn/NativeStock, pp. 9, 13, 23, 25; Angel Wynn/DanitaDelimont.com/"Danita Delimont Photography"/Newscom, pp. 11, 17; Christopher Seufert/Shutterstock Images, p. 19; Engraving by Kean Collection/Getty Images, p. 27; Image courtesy of the Stan Murphy Family/Martha's Vineyard Museum, p. 21; Joseph Prezioso/AFP via Getty Images, p. 29; National Museum of the American Indian, Smithsonian Institution (18/4443). Photo By NMAI Photo Services, p.15; Rolf_52/Shutterstock Images, p. 5

Library of Congress Control Number: 2024938824

Publisher's Cataloging-in-Publication Data
Names: Bird, F.A., author.
Title: Wampanoag / by F.A. Bird
Description: Minneapolis, Minnesota : ABDO Publishing, 2025 | Series: Native American nations | Includes online resources and index.
Identifiers: ISBN 9781098296285 (lib. bdg.) | ISBN 9798384917397 (ebook)
Subjects: LCSH: Wampanoag Indians--Juvenile literature. | Massasoit Indians--Juvenile literature. | Pokanoket Indians--Juvenile literature. | Native Americans--Juvenile literature. | Indians of North America--Juvenile literature. | Indigenous peoples--Social life and customs--Juvenile literature. | Cultural anthropology--Juvenile literature.
Classification: DDC 973.0497--dc23

Contents

Homelands	4
Society	6
Homes	8
Food	10
Clothing	12
Crafts	14
Family	16
Children	18
Traditions	20
War	22
Contact with Europeans	24
Metacom	26
The Wampanoag Today	28
Glossary	30
Online Resources	31
Index	32

CHAPTER 1

Homelands

The Wampanoag (WOM-puh-nog) lived on the eastern coast of North America. So, the Wampanoag were one of the first peoples to see the sun rise every morning. The name *Wampanoag* means "People of the First Light," or "People of the Dawn." The people spoke Wampanoag, a language in the Algonquian language family.

The Wampanoag homelands stretched from east of Narragansett Bay to the Atlantic Ocean. The lands included what is now eastern Rhode Island and southern Massachusetts. The islands of Nantucket and Martha's Vineyard were also Wampanoag lands.

Glaciers had provided the Wampanoag homelands with clay deposits, boulders, ponds, lakes, rivers, and bays. The inland forest had oak, maple, beech, birch, and evergreen trees. The shores held marshes, dunes, and sandy shorelines. The islands were combinations of shorelines, hills, marshes, and wooded areas.

The multicolored Aquinnah Cliffs at Martha's Vineyard in Massachusetts are sacred to the Wampanoag.

CHAPTER 2
Society

Wampanoag society was very close. The people depended on one another for survival. They lived together in many villages. Each village had its own chief, subchief, and Council of Elders. They were elected by the people. A chief led by **consensus**. The entire village met with the chiefs and Council of Elders to come to decisions.

Besides making decisions, the Council of Elders also gave advice and kept the history of the people. The people often met with the elders to learn about Wampanoag traditions and to hear stories.

Wampanoag religious leaders were called *powwaws*. *Powwaws* offered prayers, conducted **rituals** in sweat lodges, and led spiritual ceremonies. Some people say that the word *powwow* came from the word *powwaw*.

The Wampanoag also held seasonal ceremonies that gave thanks for many things. During these ceremonies, the community came together to sing songs, dance, and eat.

CHAPTER 3

Homes

Wampanoag homes were dome-shaped wigwams. They called this style of home a *wetu* (WE-too). Building a *wetu* took the skills of both men and women. The men built the frame, and the women covered it.

The Wampanoag men began by cutting down many young trees. Next, they dug a circular pit about 12 inches (30 cm) deep in the ground. The pit was the floor of the *wetu*. The men bent sapling poles over the pit. They tied the poles together with plant fibers. This formed a dome.

After men built the frame, Wampanoag women wove mats to cover it. They wove the mats with cattail reeds, bark, or animal skins, depending on the season.

When covering the frame, the Wampanoag left a hole open in the roof. The hole allowed smoke from the fire pit to escape. The *wetu* also had a door covered by a long cattail mat. The people slept on cattail-reed mats and animal furs.

Sheets of bark above a *wetu* smoke hole kept rain and snow from coming inside. The cover was moved as the direction of the wind changed.

Food

The land and water provided food for the Wampanoag. They hunted, fished, gathered, and gardened. Wampanoag men traveled inland to hunt for deer, elk, bear, and moose. Along the coast they hunted for rabbits, ducks, and geese. The men fished for many types of fish and shellfish. They also dug for clams and gathered oysters.

The Wampanoag gardens contained corn, beans, squash, and pumpkins. These gardens were planted using a method called hill planting. The Wampanoag planted corn at the top of a mound of soil. When the corn had grown a little, the people planted beans around it. Then, they planted squash around the beans and corn. Planted together, these crops help each other grow.

Besides gardening, women also gathered food. In June, women took a basket and gathered wild berries. In the fall, they gathered acorns and other nuts. They also gathered cranberries from the sandy marshland bogs.

Strawberries, clams, and cranberries were important to the Wampanoag diet.

CHAPTER 5
Clothing

The Wampanoag felt a kinship with their natural environment. They believed it was important to use every part of the animals that they had hunted. So, the people made their clothing from animal **hides** and furs.

Women wore dresses made from either deerskin or elk hide. Usually, a woman's dress was one piece of animal skin with fringes on the bottom. Men wore deerskin **breechcloths** and waist-high **leggings**. Sometimes they wore a deerskin shirt, or stretched a hide across one shoulder and tied it at the waist.

The Wampanoag wore sashes across the chest or as a belt. The people finger wove these sashes from plant fibers. Both men and women wore moccasins made from deer, elk, or moose leather.

In cold weather, the Wampanoag wore fur robes. A fur robe was worn with the fur side touching the skin. This kept the person warm.

Traditional Wampanoag clothing includes leggings, buckskin fringed shirts, and feather headdresses.

CHAPTER 6
Crafts

The Wampanoag created many practical and decorative objects. They used most of these objects in daily life. Sometimes the people decorated the objects with shells, feathers, or paint.

Men carved cups, bowls, and ladles with stone and antler tools. These items were beautifully made. The Wampanoag considered a **burl** cup or bowl a prized possession.

The people often gathered clay from local streambeds. They shaped the clay into pipes. These pipes were one piece, with a bowl and stem. Often, the Wampanoag decorated the bowl's edge with **geometric** designs.

The Wampanoag also gathered a special multicolored clay. They molded this clay into beautiful bowls, vases, and pots. Today, the Wampanoag still make vessels from the clay. Some use a potter's wheel, but others use the traditional **coil method**.

Wampanoag spoon carved from a maple burl

Chapter 7

Family

Each village in the Wampanoag community was like one extended family. Men and women contributed equally. Men hunted and fished. When not out hunting and fishing, they made or repaired tools and weapons. The men also grew tobacco. The Wampanoag smoked this tobacco in pipes and offered it in ceremonies to give thanks.

Wampanoag women planted and tended the other gardens. Women used hoes to control weeds and to prepare the soil for planting. This tool was a long piece of wood attached to a clamshell or deer bone. During the harvest, women wore pack baskets to help them carry crops. The women prepared all food for eating. They made sure to dry enough food for the winter.

Wampanoag elders also had special responsibilities in their families. They recounted history or told stories that taught **cultural** lessons. Winter story time was a great time for the family to come together.

Wampanoag society is matrilineal. This means homes belong to the women, and children are born into their mother's clan.

CHAPTER 8
Children

Wampanoag children played many games. They also helped with village chores, such as gathering clams. To find some types of clams, the children looked for air holes in the sand. Once they found the clams, the children dug them out from beneath the sand with a stick or large shell.

Wampanoag children gathered quahog (KOH-hawg) clams in the water. Older children waded into the water, felt in the mud with their feet, then reached down to scoop up the clam. These were used for delicious clam chowder.

Boys learned to make fishing spears and traps. They learned how to fish with these tools. Boys also helped the men set up wooden fences in a way that drove deer and small **game** to where hunters were waiting.

Wampanoag girls helped care for the younger children. They helped make clothing and prepare food. Girls also learned how to hill plant. Learning these skills helped prepare them for adulthood.

Wampanoag children are raised with respect for nature. Clams are first used for food. Then every other part is used. There should be no waste.

CHAPTER 9
Traditions

The Wampanoag told many stories about Moshup. He was a giant who lived a long time ago. Moshup was a man of peace and great wisdom. He loved to sit on a big rock and think. Some people say that his rock seat can still be found in Wampanoag territory.

Moshup loved whale meat. He would wade into the ocean and catch whales with one hand. Moshup shared his whale meat with the Wampanoag. He also taught them how to hunt for whales. In thanks, the Wampanoag gave Moshup all the tobacco they had grown for a season.

Moshup had a giant pipe to smoke the tobacco. When he was finished, Moshup emptied his pipe into the waters. The tobacco created the islands in Wampanoag territory.

Others say that Moshup dragged his toe across the land. The mark left by his toe filled with water, separating a piece of land from the mainland. This formed the island known as Martha's Vineyard.

Moshup catches a whale for his supper.

CHAPTER 10

War

The Wampanoag were a peace-loving people who did not go to war often. But, sometimes fighting became necessary to protect their hunting and fishing territories. However, the fighting did not always end in death. Sometimes the Wampanoag just **harassed trespassers** until they left.

When the Wampanoag did go to war, they fought with many of the same weapons they used to hunt. In close combat, the Wampanoag fought with war clubs and knives. The knives were usually made from quartz, flint, or bone.

For more distant fighting, the Wampanoag fought with bows and arrows. They chose the wood for the bow carefully. They twisted plant fibers to create the bowstring. The arrows had stone or bone tips.

A stone ax for cutting down trees could also be used as a war club during battle.

CHAPTER 11

Contact with Europeans

The Wampanoag first met Europeans around 1600. In the early 1600s, Squanto, a man of the Patuxet tribe, was captured and sold as a slave in Spain. He escaped to England, where he learned to speak English. When Squanto returned to his homeland, most of his people had died. So, he joined a group of Wampanoag living nearby.

In 1620, Pilgrims arrived in Wampanoag territory. They were settlers from England. They were not equipped to survive, and many died. In 1621, Squanto and Massasoit, grand **sachem** of the Wampanoag, met the Pilgrims. Squanto spoke English, so he was an interpreter. They taught the Pilgrims many things.

Tensions increased as more colonists arrived. They wanted land. They let their livestock wander. Soon, cows and pigs were destroying Wampanoag gardens.

Wampanoag Chief Massasoit meets the English in 1621.

Metacom

Metacom was a famous Wampanoag chief who was born around 1640. He was the son of Chief Massasoit. He grew up watching his father help the Pilgrims survive. Massasoit died in 1661. His first son, Wamsutta, became chief. But, Wamsutta died a year later. Then Metacom became chief.

By this time, problems had begun. The English wanted more Wampanoag land for settlement. However, land was owned by the village. An individual had no right to sell what belonged to the village. Yet soon individuals were trading Wampanoag land for blankets and guns.

Metacom and his people decided war was necessary to protect their people, land, and way of life. He joined with neighboring tribes to drive out the colonists. Today, this effort is known as King Philip's War. The colonists killed Metacom and many other native people. Several tribes were nearly wiped out. After this, European settlers were able to move west with less resistance.

Metacom was called King Philip by the English. They mistakenly thought native leaders ruled the way kings did in England.

The Wampanoag Today

Today, many Wampanoag still live within their traditional homelands. There are two **federally recognized** tribes located in Massachusetts. The Wampanoag Tribe of Gay Head (Aquinnah) has more than 1,300 members. They are located at Aquinnah, on Martha's Vineyard. The Mashpee Wampanoag Tribe is located on Cape Cod. They have 3,200 enrolled citizens.

The Wampanoag still hold seasonal ceremonies to give thanks. In August, the Wampanoag hold a Moshup festival. In October, they gather for Cranberry Day, a celebration of food, stories, and other **cultural** activities.

In the past, some people have mistakenly thought the Wampanoag were extinct. The Wampanoag want others to know they still exist, and how their people were important in the history of America.

Mashpee Wampanoag Pow Wow Princess dances at Indigenous Peoples Day in Newton, Massachusetts.

Glossary

breechcloth—a piece of hide or cloth, usually worn by men, that is wrapped between the legs and tied with a belt around the waist.

burl—a hard, rounded woody growth on a tree.

coil method—clay rolled into long ropes that are laid on top of each other in coils to make a pot.

consensus—an agreement reached by people in a group.

culture—the customs, arts, and tools of a nation or people at a certain time.

federal recognition—the US government's recognition of a tribe as being an independent nation. The tribe is eligible for special funding and protection of its lands.

game—wild animals hunted for food or sport.

geometric—made up of straight lines, circles, and other simple shapes.

harass—to continue to bother someone again and again over a period of time.

hide—an animal skin that is often thick and heavy.

leggings—coverings for the legs, usually made of cloth or leather.

ritual—a form or order to a ceremony.

sachem—a North American native chief.

trespass—to enter into the land of another without permission.

ONLINE RESOURCES

To learn more about the Wampanoag, please visit **abdobooklinks.com** or scan this QR code. These links are routinely monitored and updated to provide the most current information available.

Index

Atlantic Ocean 4

Cape Cod 28
ceremonies 6, 16, 28
chiefs 6, 24, 26
children 18
clay 4, 14
clothing 12, 18
crafts 14

elders 6, 16
Europeans 24, 26

family 16
fishing 10, 16, 18, 22
food 10, 14, 16, 18, 20, 28

gardening 10, 16, 24
gathering 10, 14, 18

homelands 4, 20, 22, 24, 26, 28
homes 8
hunting 10, 12, 16, 18, 20, 22

language 4, 24

Martha's Vineyard 4, 20, 28
Massasoit 24, 26
Metacom 26

Nantucket Island 4
Narragansett Bay 4
North America 4

Patuxet Indians 24
Pilgrims 24, 26
powwaws 6

Squanto 24
stories 6, 16, 20, 28

tobacco 16, 20
tools 10, 12, 14, 16, 18

villages 6, 16, 18, 26

Wamsutta 26
war 22, 26
weapons 16, 22